Special Forces

Henry Brook

Illustrated by Staz Johnson

Technical illustrations by Adrian Roots and Adrian Dean

Designed by Helen Edmonds,
Anna Gould and Zoe Wray

Edited by Alex Frith
Special Forces expert: Ian Maine, Royal Marines Museum

Contents

A joint US-UK Special Forces team waits to board a Black Hawk helicopter during an operation in Afghanistan in 2012.

Who are Special Forces?

Special Forces, often known as SF, are elite troops who work alone or in small teams to complete dangerous missions.

Secret armies

Most branches of the military have their own SF fighting units. Here are some famous examples from around the world.

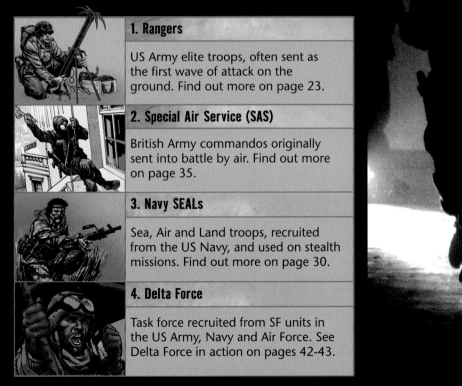

1. Rangers

US Army elite troops, often sent as the first wave of attack on the ground. Find out more on page 23.

2. Special Air Service (SAS)

British Army commandos originally sent into battle by air. Find out more on page 35.

3. Navy SEALs

Sea, Air and Land troops, recruited from the US Navy, and used on stealth missions. Find out more on page 30.

4. Delta Force

Task force recruited from SF units in the US Army, Navy and Air Force. See Delta Force in action on pages 42-43.

5. ComSubIn – Italian commando frogmen

Elite sailors from the Italian Navy, the world's oldest underwater demolition team. Find out about the team's early years on page 22.

6. Sayaret

Israeli Special Forces. In Hebrew, *sayeret* means reconnaissance, but Sayeret teams complete all kinds of missions. Find out more on page 12.

This SAS unit is charging into a compound at night as part of a training exercise.

SF soldiers are expected to have almost superhuman fighting spirit, stamina and determination.

Any mission, any time, anywhere

SF troops have to be ready to make raids and tactical strikes all over the globe, from icy mountains to barren deserts and sweltering jungles, almost always in enemy territory.

SF missions
• **Daring raids on enemy positions**
• **Observation or reconnaissance missions**
• **Sniper operations in dangerous locations**   Snipers are soldiers trained to shoot targets from far away. Find out more on page 18.
• **Counter terrorism**   Find out more on page 12.
• **Hostage rescue operations**   Read real life accounts on pages 13 and 36.

Masters of war

Some SF teams, such as the US Green Berets, were set up to train resistance groups – soldiers in other countries who are fighting against their own rulers. This is known as *unconventional warfare.*

A British Army Pathfinder Platoon team on a woodland patrol

Special training

SF units are deployed on missions that require small teams of expert soldiers, often trained for particular jobs.

This trooper is learning how to abseil, or rappel, down the side of a mountain. Using ropes to climb up or down is often known as *roping*.

SF soldiers are often known as *commandos*.

Group skills

Getting in and out of combat areas is one of the main parts of any mission, known as *insertion* and *extraction*. Most SF troops need to learn techniques such as:

- Parachute jumping
- Mountain climbing
- Deep sea diving
- Roping from helicopters
- Wilderness survival

Individual skills

Many SF soldiers choose to learn special skills to set themselves apart, such as:

- Mixed martial arts
- Setting and dismantling explosives, known as demolition
- Combat driving
- Learning foreign languages

An All Terrain
Vehicle (ATV)
provides support.
Find out more
on page 55.

Mask to protect
trooper from
dust and heat

Behind enemy lines

SF teams are often sent to map and observe targets deep in enemy territory. This is known as reconnaissance, or *recon*.

This unit is part of the Australian Army Special Operations Task Group, seen here on a recon patrol in Afghanistan in 2006.

Sniffer dog, trained to find hidden explosives

This patrol is arranged in a jagged line, with each trooper looking in a different direction.

Assault rifle, a weapon used in general combat

Arctic action

Many British SF teams are sent to icy north Norway for cold weather training. Experts from the Royal Marines, known as Mountain Leaders, teach them rock climbing, polar survival skills and long-distance skiing.

All Royal Marines have to complete arctic training. Although they are not classed as Special Forces by the British Army, Royal Marines are trained to similar high standards.

The French Foreign Legion also undertake ski training. This photo shows a Foreign Legion platoon trekking across the French Alps.

Planning for the worst

To learn how to survive a sudden break in thin ice, soldiers drop into freezing water wearing a pack and skis. They only have seconds to climb out and change into dry clothes to avoid deadly hypothermia.

Fighting terror

Many Special Forces units are tasked with protecting their country from criminals and terrorist groups. This is known as counter terrorism.

Sayeret Matkal (special reconaissance unit)
(Israel, 1962–present)

Specialist missions:
- Counter terrorism
- Hostage rescue
- Gathering intelligence

Israel's SF units, such as the Sayeret, are world leaders in counter terrorism.

Uzi submachine gun

Assault vest with pouches to hold spare ammunition, smoke grenades and medical supplies

Submachine guns are light, short-barrelled weapons that fire a high rate of bullets.

Operation Thunderbolt

DATE: 4th July, 1976

LOCATION: Entebbe airport, Uganda

SITUATION: A plane flying out of Israel has been hijacked, and the passengers are being held hostage in the airport at Entebbe, Uganda. The Ugandan military has agreed to protect the hijackers.

Entebbe airport
Terminal building

Ugandan planes and soldiers

MISSION: Israeli commandos, led by a squad of Sayeret Matkal troopers, are sent in to rescue the hostages.

The commandos arrive in a large transport plane. They hide inside three cars, disguised as a convoy carrying the Ugandan president – due to fly back from a visit abroad.

At first, the disguise works...

...but a guard gets suspicious, and a soldier is forced to open fire.

The commandos leap out and storm into the terminal building.

Within minutes all the hijackers are dead and the commandos are rushing the hostages onto the transport plane.

A second unit of commandos forms a defensive ring around the transport plane, and fends off the Ugandan soldiers with rockets and grenades. The rescue plane takes off. Four hostages and one commando lose their lives during the operation.

Special Forces long ago

Since ancient times small teams of elite troops have helped large armies to win vital battles. Here are some of the finest examples.

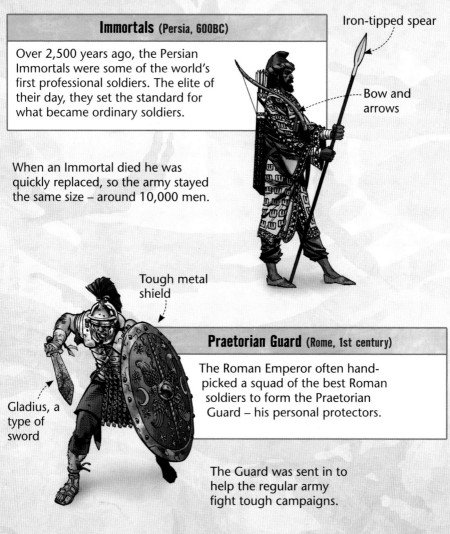

Immortals (Persia, 600BC)

Over 2,500 years ago, the Persian Immortals were some of the world's first professional soldiers. The elite of their day, they set the standard for what became ordinary soldiers.

When an Immortal died he was quickly replaced, so the army stayed the same size – around 10,000 men.

Iron-tipped spear

Bow and arrows

Tough metal shield

Gladius, a type of sword

Praetorian Guard (Rome, 1st century)

The Roman Emperor often hand-picked a squad of the best Roman soldiers to form the Praetorian Guard – his personal protectors.

The Guard was sent in to help the regular army fight tough campaigns.

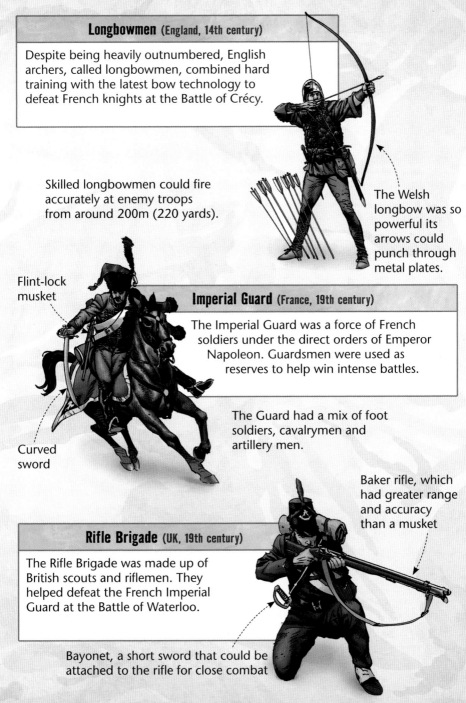

Longbowmen (England, 14th century)

Despite being heavily outnumbered, English archers, called longbowmen, combined hard training with the latest bow technology to defeat French knights at the Battle of Crécy.

Skilled longbowmen could fire accurately at enemy troops from around 200m (220 yards).

The Welsh longbow was so powerful its arrows could punch through metal plates.

Flint-lock musket

Imperial Guard (France, 19th century)

The Imperial Guard was a force of French soldiers under the direct orders of Emperor Napoleon. Guardsmen were used as reserves to help win intense battles.

The Guard had a mix of foot soldiers, cavalrymen and artillery men.

Curved sword

Baker rifle, which had greater range and accuracy than a musket

Rifle Brigade (UK, 19th century)

The Rifle Brigade was made up of British scouts and riflemen. They helped defeat the French Imperial Guard at the Battle of Waterloo.

Bayonet, a short sword that could be attached to the rifle for close combat

Trackers and hunters

A hundred years ago, many Special Forces soldiers were drawn from communities where people grew up learning bushcraft skills, such as tracking prey and using camouflage.

This soldier is wearing a *ghillie suit* – a camouflage outfit originally designed by hunters – made from strips of cloth, twigs and leaves.

To find soldiers wearing ghillie suits, enemy search squads need cameras that pick up heat signals.

Kommandos (South Africa, 1880–1902)

In the 1880s, Afrikaans-speaking European settlers in South Africa, known as *boers*, began a long fight for independence from Great Britain.

In Afrikaans, the word *kommando* means 'cavalry unit'. The British army later adopted the word 'commando' to describe their first official SF unit.

Lovat Scouts (UK, 1900–present)

Gamekeepers from the Scottish highlands, known as *ghillies*, were chosen to form an army regiment called the Lovat Scouts.

The Lovat Scouts used their hunting skills on sniper missions in the First World War.

Gurkhas (UK, 1817–present)

The Gurkha people from the mountains of Nepal have been fighting as part of the British Army for almost 200 years.

Gurkhas all carry a curved machete called a kukri. Used as a multi-purpose farming tool in Nepal, it makes a fearsome weapon.

17

Sharpshooters

Soldiers trained to identify and take out distant targets are known as *snipers*. The best can stalk and shoot enemy soldiers and equipment up to a mile away.

Sharpshooters often work in pairs. The sniper, who shoots, is accompanied by a *spotter*, who helps the sniper aim accurately, and defends from surprise attacks.

A German sniper team in Afghanistan in 2008

Spotter using binoculars

Fact finding

Trained snipers who join SF teams are often sent on recon missions. They use their camouflage skills and powerful rifle sights to watch what the enemy is up to without being seen.

Telescopic, all-weather sight

Sniper holding a long range rifle

A bipod rest keeps the gun steady.

Sniper hides

Some sniper teams need to make a hiding place, or *hide*, and wait there for days.

First, they dig a shallow trench and carefully cover it with turf, netting and foliage.

Then they collect all the earth and take it far away to conceal any trace of their location.

The sniper slots his gun through holes in the turf, keeping his head and body inside the hide.

Trench warriors

Much of the First World War (1914-18) was fought in muddy trenches and tunnels. Faced with hidden machine guns, it was impossible for large armies to move across open ground – so leaders created small units instead.

Stick grenade, a German explosive that could be thrown further than the British pineapple-shaped hand grenade

Stormtroopers

The German Army set up a crack unit to take control of enemy trenches. These early SF soldiers were known as *Stosstruppen*, or stormtroopers.

A German stormtrooper hurls a stick grenade, the first stage of a raid on an enemy trench.

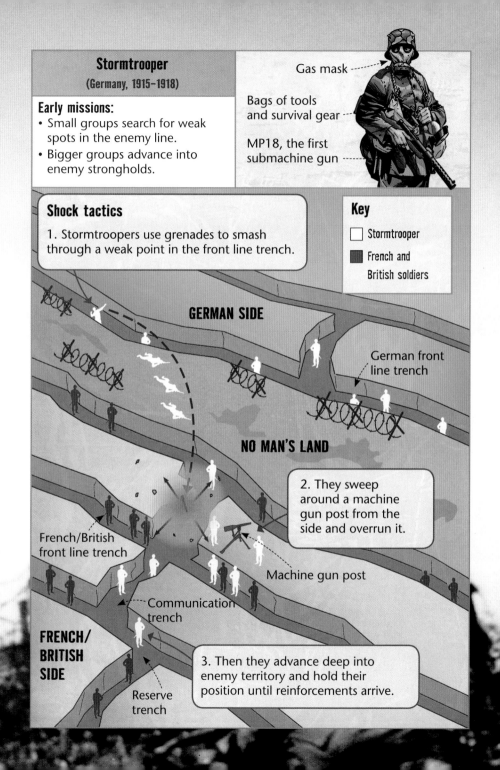

Stormtrooper
(Germany, 1915–1918)

Early missions:
- Small groups search for weak spots in the enemy line.
- Bigger groups advance into enemy strongholds.

Gas mask

Bags of tools and survival gear

MP18, the first submachine gun

Shock tactics

1. Stormtroopers use grenades to smash through a weak point in the front line trench.

Key

☐ Stormtrooper

◼ French and British soldiers

GERMAN SIDE

German front line trench

NO MAN'S LAND

2. They sweep around a machine gun post from the side and overrun it.

French/British front line trench

Machine gun post

Communication trench

FRENCH/ BRITISH SIDE

3. Then they advance deep into enemy territory and hold their position until reinforcements arrive.

Reserve trench

The Second World War

The all-terrain, all-climate conflict of the Second World War demanded new classes of elite soldiers. Many are still in service today.

Commando (UK, 1940–present)

Early missions:
- Clearing minefields
- Demolition
- Reconnaissance
- Small scale raids into enemy territory

Climbing rope

Green beret

Mills bomb

Bren machine gun

Commandos are drawn from the Army, Navy and Air Force.

Khaki uniform

Goggles

Magnetic mine

MAS frogmen sank over 20 ships during the course of the War.

Decima Flottiglia MAS

(Italy, 1936–1945)

Early missions:
- Piloting underwater torpedoes
- Attaching mines to enemy ships
- Cutting through protective netting around enemy ports

Respirator

Air tank

Fallschirmjäger
(Germany, 1936–1945)

Early missions:
- Parachuting into enemy territory
- Raiding key targets
- Holding onto enemy territory until back-up forces arrive

Steel helmet

MP40 submachine gun

Overalls to protect from wind

Helmet and goggles

Launcher to fire grappling hook

Rangers (USA, 1943–present)

Early missions:
- Raiding key targets
- Holding onto enemy territory until back-up forces arrive

Osnaz (USSR, 1941–1945)

Early missions:
- Scouting behind enemy lines
- Sabotaging missions on enemy railways and army bases
- Sniper duty

Osnaz troops were part of a unit known as the 'Special Purpose Motorized Rifle Brigade'.

Snow camouflage

Sniper rifle

Binoculars

Parachute raids

Very early in the War, German leaders combined stormtrooper tactics with air transport and created a new fighting force. These elite soldiers, known as *paratroopers*, jumped directly onto key targets, far in advance of the main army.

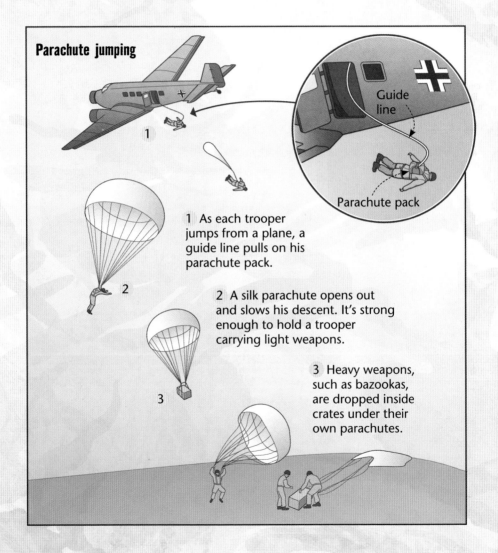

Parachute jumping

Guide line

Parachute pack

1 As each trooper jumps from a plane, a guide line pulls on his parachute pack.

2 A silk parachute opens out and slows his descent. It's strong enough to hold a trooper carrying light weapons.

3 Heavy weapons, such as bazookas, are dropped inside crates under their own parachutes.

Sky soldiers

The Allied Nations, including Britain and the USA, quickly set up their own paratrooper units known as *airborne forces*.

A soldier from the Parachute Regiment of the British Army lands after a test jump in 1942.

The impact of a parachute landing is the same as jumping from a 3m (10ft) wall.

These volunteers are training to be Commandos during the Second World War. They learn how to climb cliffs, crawl along ropes, land from small boats and plant explosives – all while under live fire from instructors.

Churchill's leopards

In 1940, British soldiers saw posters asking for volunteers to join a new type of combat unit – the Commandos. The country's prime minister, Winston Churchill, described these men as, "leopards, ready to spring at the throats of the enemy."

Royal Marine commandos

Most commandos in Britain today serve within 3 Commando Brigade, part of the UK Royal Marines.

Commandos often apply camouflage cream before a mission. This stops skin from shining in moonlight, and protects against insects.

Rangers take the cliffs

DATE: June 6, 1944 – known as D-Day

LOCATION: Pointe-du-Hoc, Normandy, northern France

SITUATION: The countries fighting Germany have raised a huge force to invade German-occupied France. Thousands of troops, including battalions of US Army Rangers, are poised to charge onto the beaches of Normandy.

Main road

THE MISSION: To destroy heavy artillery (anti-ship guns) on the cliff top known as Pointe-du-Hoc, and take control of the main road.

Barbed wire

Minefield

Gun emplacements – craters that hold artillery

Sniper hideouts, known as pillboxes

Pointe-du-Hoc

Landing ships

English Channel

Around 07:10, 225 Rangers reach the Pointe. German soldiers drop grenades, and fire down from the cliffs with machine guns.

The rangers use grappling hooks to attach ropes and ladders to the cliff, and begin to ascend.

Those who survive the 30m (100ft) climb then fight for every step of the Pointe.

Rangers are trained to keep advancing even under fire, a tactic that terrifies the enemy.

By 07:45, the rangers have taken control of the cliffs. A radio operator on the beach sends a coded message to the main invasion force.

But the mission isn't complete. 50 rangers push ahead to the road, still under heavy fire. Meanwhile, two men destroy the German anti-ship guns with metal-melting grenades.

For the next two days, the surviving rangers hold the road and the cliff. They keep the Germans from firing on the main invasion force on the beaches below, helping ensure their victory. When the battle ends, 90 men remain fit to fight.

Navy marauders

In 1962 the US Navy formed a special unit that could be inserted into battle from Sea, Air or Land – the SEALs. The unit's first combat missions were to make daring recon patrols into enemy territory during the Vietnam War.

US Navy SEALs
(USA, 1962–present)

Specialist missions:
- Mapping coastal targets
- Clearing underwater obstacles
- Gathering intelligence

Early enemies named them 'greenfaces' because of the camouflage paint they wore.

Semi-automatic pistol

Stoner 63 assault rifle, a light rifle with the firepower of a heavy machine gun

Staying silent

SEALs often attach a suppressor, or silencer, to their pistols. This deadens and changes the sound of a gunshot, making it harder for the enemy to identify their position.

SEALs choose their own combat clothes. In Vietnam, many wore tigerstripe camouflage clothing to break up their outline in thick jungle.

Stealth patrols

After insertion, SEALs advance in a formation designed for maximum safety and firepower.

'Tail-End Charlie' protects the rear.

Each soldier points eyes and guns in different directions.

'Pointman' watches for tripwires and enemy activity ahead.

Tunnel raiders

DATE: 1963-1969

LOCATION: The jungles of Vietnam

SITUATION: The Vietnam War (1955-1975) was a savage conflict between rival armies in the north and south of the country. In 1962, the US Army joined the War, backing the armies of the south.

THE MISSION: Special Forces units must find and destroy underground bases used by the enemy – the Viet Cong.

NORTH VIETNAM

CHINA

LAOS

THAILAND

CAMBODIA

SOUTH VIETNAM

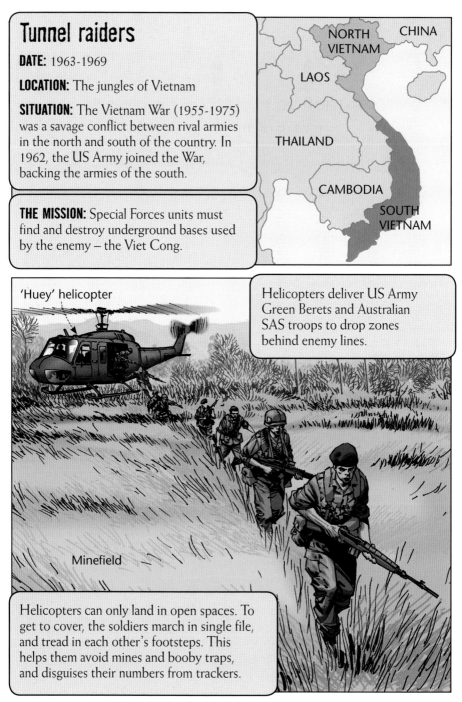

'Huey' helicopter

Helicopters deliver US Army Green Berets and Australian SAS troops to drop zones behind enemy lines.

Minefield

Helicopters can only land in open spaces. To get to cover, the soldiers march in single file, and tread in each other's footsteps. This helps them avoid mines and booby traps, and disguises their numbers from trackers.

The Viet Cong dug hundreds of tunnel networks in the jungle floor, to store weapons and to shelter from American bomber raids.

Firing post

Snake trap

Sleeping area

Kitchen

Ammunition store

Tunnels are protected by guards and booby traps — including snakes tied to the roof by their tails.

The soldiers meet local informants, who show them hidden trapdoors that lead into the tunnels.

Soldiers crawl through the tunnels taking prisoners and searching for maps and weapons.

When the tunnels are clear they seal them with explosives.

Black Kit

British SAS units take on secret, or *stealth*, missions all over the world. For raids on buildings or missions in urban areas they wear flameproof stealth uniform known as Black Kit.

Respirator filters out smoke and gas

Dark goggles shield eyes from flashes

Flame-proof hood

Semi-automatic pistol

Gloves

Knife pouch

Hooks and straps for flash grenades, smoke grenades and stun grenades

Helmet (worn beneath hood)
- Made from kevlar, a mesh tougher than steel that can stop some bullets
- Contains built-in video camera and communications array

Assault vest padded with bulletproof plates

Belt doubles as a harness for roping

Black, flameproof overalls

Kneepads

Weapons
- Semi-automatic pistol
- Sledgehammer
- Submachine gun
- Knife

Light but tough assault boots

A light is attached to the gun barrel.

Stun grenade

Black Kit, developed in the 1970s, has been copied by Special Forces teams all around the world.

SAS
(Britain, 1950–present)

Specialist missions:
- Recon behind enemy lines
- Counter terrorist raids
- Insertion directly into combat zones, often by parachute

Go, go, go!

DATE: May, 1980

LOCATION: Iranian Embassy, London

SITUATION: A week ago, six armed intruders entered the embassy and took the staff hostage. Since then, one hostage has been killed.

THE MISSION: The SAS have been planning a raid for five days. Using listening devices, they have plotted the likely positions of the 25 hostages.

One squad triggers a decoy explosion on the roof of the building...

...while another team blasts its way through the windows in front...

The Iranian embassy building

Front entrance

...and a third team uses sledgehammers to smash through the rear door.

As soon as the explosions begin, the SAS rope down the rear of the building and smash their way in through a window.

The troops use shotguns to blow open doors. They throw in loud stun grenades to startle people, and smoke grenades to spread confusion.

SAS troops form a chain down the stairwell, and bundle the hostages out of the rear door.

The raid ends in just 11 minutes. All but one of the hostages were rescued. During the raid, five of the six intruders were killed, and one SAS soldier was seriously wounded.

In the kill house

SF units train for urban combat in purpose-built compounds known as *shoot houses* or *kill houses*. Inside, teams rehearse raids in darkness using live ammunition, and learn how to clear rooms of any threats.

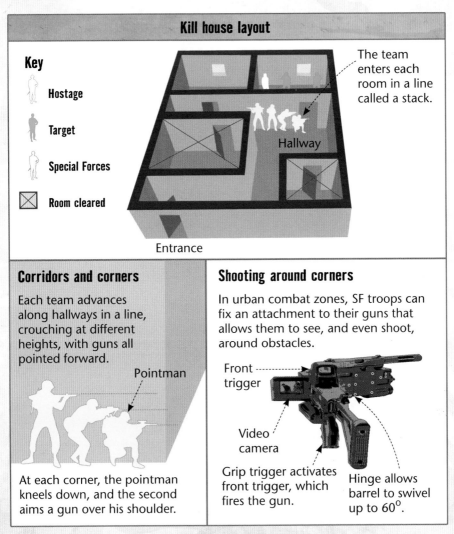

Kill house layout

Key

- Hostage
- Target
- Special Forces
- Room cleared

The team enters each room in a line called a stack.

Hallway

Entrance

Corridors and corners

Each team advances along hallways in a line, crouching at different heights, with guns all pointed forward.

Pointman

At each corner, the pointman kneels down, and the second aims a gun over his shoulder.

Shooting around corners

In urban combat zones, SF troops can fix an attachment to their guns that allows them to see, and even shoot, around obstacles.

Front trigger

Video camera

Grip trigger activates front trigger, which fires the gun.

Hinge allows barrel to swivel up to 60°.

Instructors watch from a viewing platform above each room.

These soldiers are running a room-clearing drill in a shoot house in Grafenwoehr training complex in Bavaria, Germany.

US unit Delta Force build their own kill houses based on plans for actual buildings they will have to raid on future missions.

Sand racers

Special Forces patrols sacrifice protection for speed. On hit-and-run raids in the desert, they zip across the sand in stripped-down vehicles nicknamed 'dune buggies'.

Seat for gunner at the top

Mounted heavy machine gun

Light strike vehicle

- **Top speed on sand:** 110km/h (70mph)
- **Can hold:** 4 soldiers
- **Used by:** US SF on desert patrols

The latest dune buggies are officially known as 'Light Strike Vehicles'.

Anti-tank rocket launcher

Supacat Jackal

- **Top speed on sand:** 80km/h (50mph)
- **Can hold:** 5 soldiers
- **Used by:** UK SF on recon missions

The Jackal is used by the British Army and the Australian SAS. As well as crew, it can hold food, weapons and other vital equipment for long missions.

SAND-X ATV

- **Top speed on sand:** 185km/h (115mph)
- **Can hold:** 1 soldier
- **Used by:** US SF on solo missions

Tracks on the rear can cross almost any terrain, from sand to snow.

Scud hunters

DATE: 1991

LOCATION: Western desert of Iraq

SITUATION: In August 1990, Iraq invaded the small nation of Kuwait. By January 1991, the US Army was poised to lead a force of allied countries to free Kuwait.

IRAQ

THE MISSION: Delta Force and SAS teams in dune buggies cross the Iraqi border, searching for scud missile trucks that have fired on their allies.

KUWAIT

SAUDI ARABIA

Here, an SAS team has hidden their buggy in camouflage nets while they watch a road...

Scud missiles can attack targets up to 300km (190 miles) away.

Camouflage netting

...until they spot a missile truck through the sights on their sniper rifles.

It's a lone truck, so the team can take it out themselves with a bazooka.

The explosion will alert enemy forces, so the team moves out quickly.

Meanwhile, the Delta Force team has intercepted a convoy. One trooper contacts his commanders to send in an air strike...

...Laser designator

...while another uses a device called a designator to bounce a laser off the lead vehicle.

Fighter planes track the laser and drop bombs onto the convoy...

...while the team races away.

If the buggy breaks down, the team can use mini radios to request emergency rescue. They fix a rendezvous point...

...so helicopter pilots can quickly extract them.

Night vision goggles are designed to show a green image. This is because the human eye can see many different shades of green.

A carbine – a type of gun used by SF soldiers for close combat in cities and jungles

This photo of a soldier wearing night vision goggles was taken using a camera with a night vision lens.

Night hunters

Special Forces often attack under cover of darkness, using night vision goggles to give them a clear view. The goggles boost weak sources of light to project a clear image into the soldier's eye.

Seeing in the dark

In zero light areas, such as tunnels, soldiers use thermal sights that convert heat into pictures.

Thermal sights show hot shapes, such as bodies, engines and firing guns, as bright patches on a dark background.

Laser rangefinder beams help the shooter judge distance to targets.

Manhunt

DATE: 2010-2011

LOCATION: Abbottabad, Pakistan

BACKGROUND: In September 2001, Osama bin Laden masterminded a series of deadly attacks against the USA. US Special Forces have been hunting him ever since. Finally, in September 2010, they get a promising lead...

US Secret Service agents in Pakistan intercept a phone call from a messenger believed to work for bin Laden. They follow his car to a compound in the city of Abbottabad.

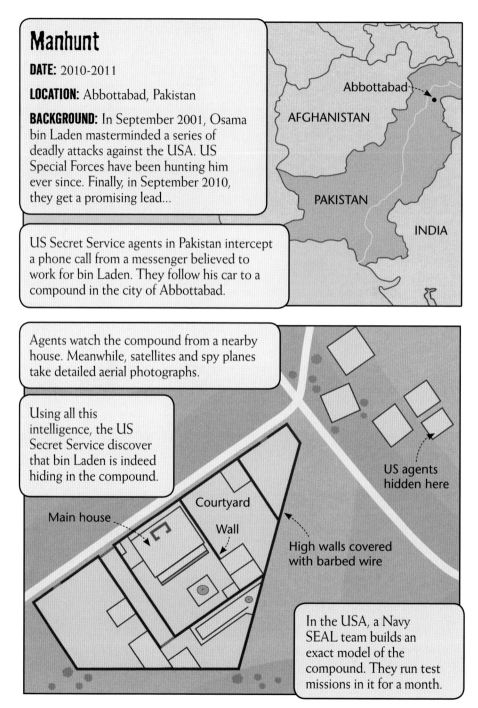

Abbottabad

AFGHANISTAN

PAKISTAN

INDIA

Agents watch the compound from a nearby house. Meanwhile, satellites and spy planes take detailed aerial photographs.

Using all this intelligence, the US Secret Service discover that bin Laden is indeed hiding in the compound.

US agents hidden here

Courtyard

Main house

Wall

High walls covered with barbed wire

In the USA, a Navy SEAL team builds an exact model of the compound. They run test missions in it for a month.

THE MISSION: On May 2 2011, US President Obama gives the order for the SEAL team to storm the real compound.

They fly to Abbottabad in helicopters from an airbase in Afghanistan.

Chinook

Black Hawk

Cameras beneath the helicopters send live video footage to the mission commanders.

The insertion is not straightforward. One of the Black Hawks crash lands inside the compound...

...and the SEAL team inside is forced to leap into action from the ground, rather than roping onto the roof.

Night vision goggles

Acting quickly, the SEALs blow their way through a wall and into the main house.

After a short gun battle, bin Laden is dead.

The SEALs destroy the crashed helicopter and extract safely with bin Laden's body.

The SEAL commanders, and the President himself, watch the operation via the helicopter video cameras.

Insertion

Special Forces try to begin their missions without alerting enemy troops. This is known as *insertion*. Helicopters can carry teams most of the way, but sometimes the safest or fastest way to get onto the ground is by rope.

Rope tricks

Climbing or sliding down a rope is known as *fast roping*. Soldiers wear thick gloves to protect their hands when sliding.

US Navy SEALs rope down from a Seahawk helicopter as part of a training exercise.

Hook and line

To undertake recon missions in places where helicopters can't land, teams of soldiers are hooked to a line and carried into the area. This is known as Special Patrol Insertion/ Extraction, or SPIE.

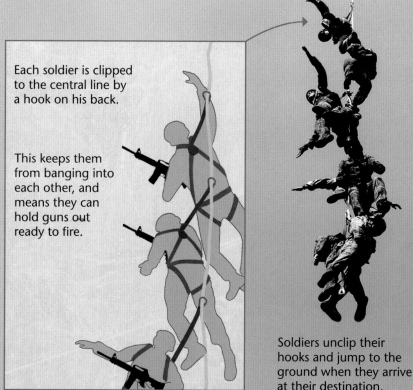

Each soldier is clipped to the central line by a hook on his back.

This keeps them from banging into each other, and means they can hold guns out ready to fire.

Soldiers unclip their hooks and jump to the ground when they arrive at their destination.

By sea

Amphibious SF units are trained to enter and exit missions by sea. They use well-protected and fully armed vessels on the open ocean and smaller, stealth craft to take them to targets on land. Small ships can be dropped into position by helicopters.

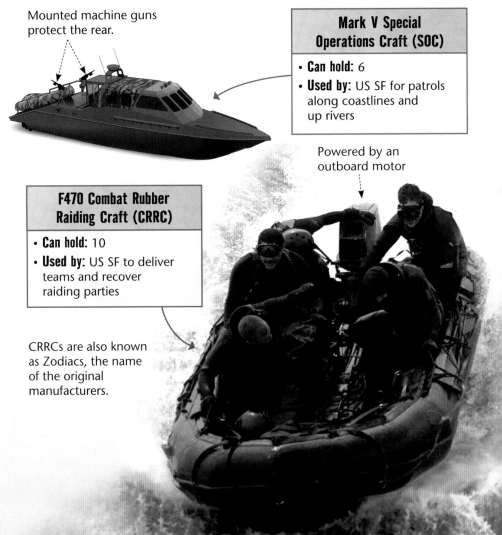

Mounted machine guns protect the rear.

Mark V Special Operations Craft (SOC)

- **Can hold:** 6
- **Used by:** US SF for patrols along coastlines and up rivers

Powered by an outboard motor

F470 Combat Rubber Raiding Craft (CRRC)

- **Can hold:** 10
- **Used by:** US SF to deliver teams and recover raiding parties

CRRCs are also known as Zodiacs, the name of the original manufacturers.

Deep cover

Many ultra-stealthy missions begin under water.
Frogmen swim or use submersibles, such as an SDV,
to attack ships or slip silently into enemy territory.

Most US submarines have
a docking station on their
deck for an SDV.

SEAL Delivery
Vehicle (SDV)

- **Can hold:** 6
- **Used by:** US Navy SEALS to
  deliver small squads for
  recon or raiding missions

By air

Land-based missions often begin with daring parachute jumps at night, right into combat zones. Two main tactics are used: HALO and HAHO.

HAHO: High Altitude, High Opening

Most HAHO jumps begin at about 10.5km (35,000ft) above the ground. Jumpers open their parachutes almost immediately.

HAHO jumpers fall separately, and steer their way to an agreed landing point, or *drop zone.*

HALO: High Altitude, Low Opening

HALO jumps can begin over 7.5km (25,000ft) above the ground. The team often jumps in one group.

HAHO and HALO jumpers are too small to be detected by enemy radar stations.

HAHO jumpers can begin their descent in neutral airspace, but land deep inside enemy territory.

HALO jumpers open their parachutes at around 600m (2,000ft). The team lands close together and can charge straight into action.

A Belgian Shepherd dog jumps with a soldier from an Austrian SF team over the mountains of Narvik, Norway.

Military dogs are calm jumpers. Unlike people, most dogs have no fear of heights.

Dog jumpers

Dogs have been making airdrops since the Second World War. They wear a special harness that clips to the paratrooper's belt. Dogs help soldiers to search tight spaces, and uncover mines buried under the ground.

By land

Troops on recon missions need to cope with rough terrain and enemy soldiers, often at high speeds.

Ground Mobility Vehicle (GMV)

- **Can hold:** 5
- **Used by:** Small teams of US SF to undertake long patrols behind enemy lines.

Machine gun

Bushmaster

- **Can hold:** 10
- **Used by:** Australian SF to transport troops into and through high-risk areas

Machine gun

Mine-proof protective plating

Tough metal shields protect the gunner from bullets.

Smoke grenade launchers

UK Royal Marines test drive a BvS-10, nicknamed 'the Viking', through a shallow river.

BvS-10 All Terrain Vehicle (ATV)

- **Can hold:** 13
- **Used by:** 3 Commando Brigade and UK SF teams to undertake long patrols behind enemy lines.

Mount for a machine gun

The Viking runs on tracks that give it incredible grip across mud, swamps and snow.

A Chinook helicopter extracts a special operations team inside a rigid-hulled inflatable boat.

Extraction

No mission is complete until the soldiers are safely back at base. When planning a raid, the Special Forces team agrees a location, called a rendezvous, where a waiting vehicle can pick them up.

Nobody left behind

One of the oldest SF rescue teams was set up by the US Air Force to find and help airmen lost in enemy territory. Known as Pararescue Jumpers, or PJs, each man is a trained medic and combat expert.

Air rescue

1 PJs in aircraft respond to a distress signal, or search for survivors from an aborted mission.

Search plane with radar dome

Distress signal

PJ teams on board

PJs can jump by parachute or reach survivors by helicopter.

2 In awkward places, such as mountainsides, the team ropes down to the ledge.

3 PJs carry injured soldiers to a spot where the aircraft can land. If that's not possible, they hoist soldiers to the helicopter on a winch.

Reserve craft hover in the air to prevent enemy troops from getting too close.

Special skills

Soldiers training for Special Forces have to be ready for any kind of mission. So they must become experts in a wide range of battle skills.

Demolition men

Explosives are a vital tool for sabotage missions, such as destroying roads, blowing up bridges, and smashing communications equipment.

Hand-to-hand combat

SF soldiers are trained to use a variety of different weapons. But they all need to know how to fight and disarm an enemy, even if they're unarmed.

Knocking an opponent to the ground

Key

 SF soldier

Opponent

1. Lean towards opponent.

2. Sweep leg behind and into the back of opponents leg.

3. Opponent topples to the ground.

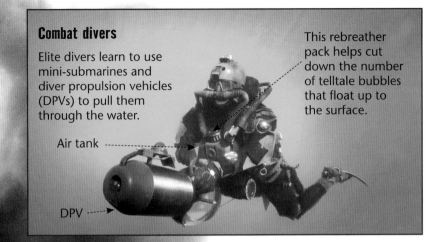

Combat divers

Elite divers learn to use mini-submarines and diver propulsion vehicles (DPVs) to pull them through the water.

This rebreather pack helps cut down the number of telltale bubbles that float up to the surface.

Air tank

DPV

A US Special Forces team demonstrates the use of plastic explosives to destroy enemy weapons in Kandahar, Afghanistan.

Silent signals

Special Forces troops try to be as quiet as possible in the field. Here are some hand signals US soldiers use to communicate with each other without making a whisper.

Freeze

A fist held at shoulder height means: 'Stand still.'

Look

Two fingers pointing at the eyes means: 'Take a good look around.'

Sniper

Making an 'O' shape around one eye means the person has spotted a sniper.

Come to me

Swirling a finger around in the air means the unit should gather together.

Showing distance

Banging fists together, then lifting a finger, shows the distance to a target ahead.

One fingers raised means 100m (or 100 yards) ahead, two fingers means 200m, and so on.

Vehicle coming

Holding a fist at chest height and moving it from side to side means a vehicle is approaching.

Take cover

A hand held open at waist height, with the palm facing down, means: 'Take cover.'

Advance

Sweeping the arm forward with an open hand means: 'Advance.'

Message received

Making an 'O' with one hand at head height means: 'I understand.'

Military alphabet

To ensure messages are correctly understood, soldiers use a name for each letter of the alphabet when spelling out code words over a radio.

NATO spelling alphabet used worldwide since 1965	US military alphabet in use from 1941-1956
Alpha	Able
Bravo	Baker
Charlie	Charlie
Delta	Dog
Echo	Easy
Foxtrot	Fox
Golf	George
Hotel	How
India	Item
Juliet	Jig
Kilo	King
Lima	Love
Mike	Mike
November	Nan
Oscar	Oboe
Papa	Peter
Quebec	Queen
Romeo	Roger
Sierra	Sugar
Tango	Tare
Uniform	Uncle
Victor	Victor
Whiskey	William
X-ray	X-ray
Yankee	Yoke
Zulu	Zebra

SF teams are often assigned names using these alphabet codes, for example *Delta* Force.

Staying alive

When a mission goes wrong, or extraction fails, SF troops rely on wilderness survival training to keep them safe.

Priority one: keep moving

The greatest danger is likely to come from enemy troops. So soldiers travel under cover of darkness, and stay on the move.

Going into a mission, SF soldiers carry up to 50kg (110lbs) of essential gear.

Priority two: build a shelter

Everyone needs to stop for rest each day. But, without warm shelter, you can die from exposure in just a few hours.

This is called a **debris shelter**.

Thick branch supports the roof.

Top layer of leaves and mulch keeps the shelter dry and warm

Smaller sticks woven together on each side

Soldiers protect their hiding places with traps, such as a grenade connected to a tripwire.

Soldier crawls in here

Priority three: find clean water

Without water you will die in about three days.

In a desert, follow animals or even insects to locate water holes.

On a mountainside, soak up morning dew with a shirt.

In the woods, squeeze water out of moss.

Priority four: find food

Without food you will die in about three weeks.

Food must be eaten raw – starting a fire to cook it might alert the enemy.

Soldiers must take care not to eat poisonous fruits.

Basic survival kit

SF troops can decide how much equipment they want to carry on each mission. Some things are more essential than others.

- **Hook and line** to catch fish
- **Signal mirror**
- **Sewing kit** to repair clothes
- **Compass**
- **First aid kit**
- **Water purifier tablets**
- **Plastic sheet** for warmth
- **Weapons and spare ammunition** – often taking up the most space

Handle

Commando saw, used to cut through branches, snare animals, or as part of a trap

Handle

Cutting edge can be coiled up to save space.

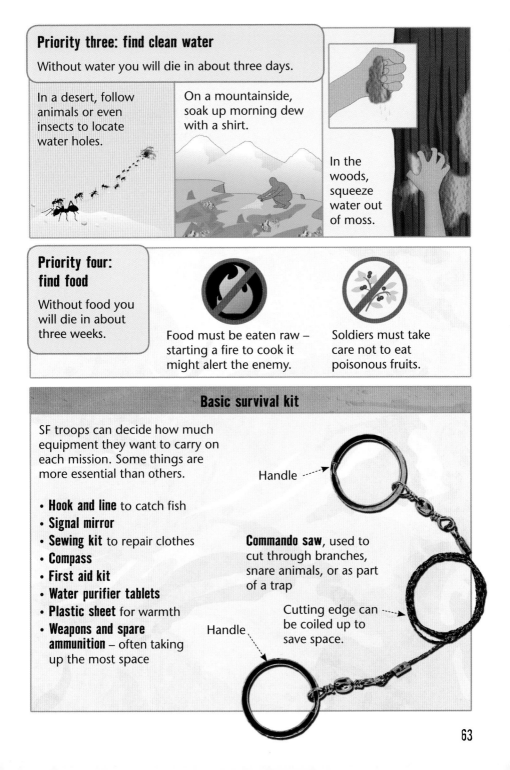

Off the battlefield

Not all members of Special Forces are serving soldiers. There are also elite units in police forces and rescue groups who work to fight crime, break up riots and prevent terrorist attacks.

A GIGN team on top of a mobile stariway vehicle in Satory, France

Submachine gun

This riot-protection helmet has a tough inner visor beneath the plastic outer visor.

GIGN (Groupe d'Intervention de la Gendarmerie Nationale)
France, 1973–present

Specialist missions:
- Counter terrorist raids
- Riot control
- Hostage rescue

Combat shotgun

Platform of a mobile stairway truck (see page 71)

Unit description	Specialist missions
Los Angeles Police Department SWAT (Special Weapons And Tactics) Los Angeles, USA, 1968–present	• Security for international events • Assisting police against heavily-armed criminal gangs
Federal Police GSG 9 (Grenzschutzgruppe 9, or Border Group 9) Germany, 1973–present	• Counter terrorist raids • Protecting high-ranking officials • Hostage rescue

Dangerous work

Some of the toughest courses for SF recruits are taught by Russian elite units known as Spetsnaz. Recruits storm into burning buildings under live fire, and are taught to control their fear and ignore pain.

Spetsnaz soldiers leap into a building during a training exercise.

AK-74 assault rifle

Spetsnaz Alfa Group
(USSR / Russia, 1974–present)

Specialist missions:
- Hostage rescue
- Charging vehicles and buildings

Siege skills

Three ways to rope down from a rooftop

Sitting down
Used for sneak attacks, and to break into windows.

Head first
Used when the soldier needs to see or aim at targets below.

Running
Used for shock attacks, one hand on rope, the other firing a gun.

Clearing an enemy vehicle

1 The first soldier throws a stun grenade into the vehicle...

...then crouches down.

2 A second soldier kneels next to first soldier.

3 Third soldier climbs over the other two and charges head first into the vehicle.

Hijack!

This scene shows how a GIGN team is trained to use a carefully synchronized attack to take control of a hijacked plane that has just landed in an airport.

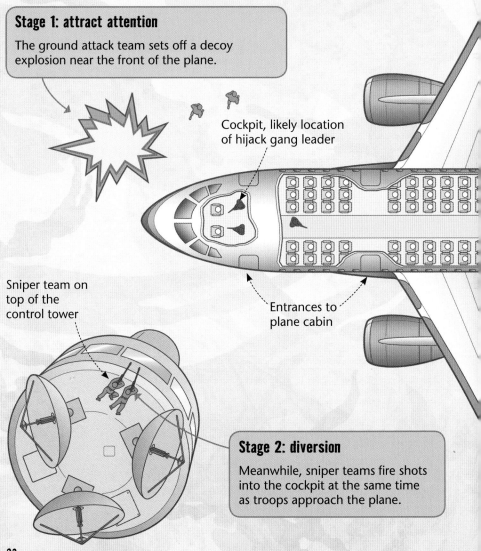

Stage 1: attract attention

The ground attack team sets off a decoy explosion near the front of the plane.

Cockpit, likely location of hijack gang leader

Sniper team on top of the control tower

Entrances to plane cabin

Stage 2: diversion

Meanwhile, sniper teams fire shots into the cockpit at the same time as troops approach the plane.

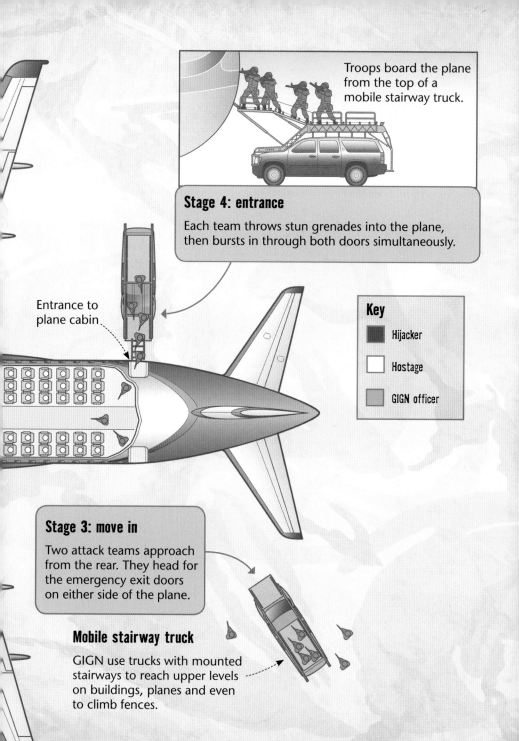

Troops board the plane from the top of a mobile stairway truck.

Stage 4: entrance

Each team throws stun grenades into the plane, then bursts in through both doors simultaneously.

Entrance to plane cabin

Key

◼	Hijacker
◻	Hostage
◼	GIGN officer

Stage 3: move in

Two attack teams approach from the rear. They head for the emergency exit doors on either side of the plane.

Mobile stairway truck

GIGN use trucks with mounted stairways to reach upper levels on buildings, planes and even to climb fences.

Joining the 10% club

The British SAS has one of the toughest selection processes in the world. Many army volunteers apply for the training, but only around 10% make it through.

Stage 1: endurance

Soldiers have to complete a 65km (40 mile) hike carrying a full pack and weapons.

Many collapse from exhaustion and pain.

Stage 2: jungle training

A small group of hopefuls is dropped in a jungle to learn how to survive in this hostile environment. Even hardened troopers give in to the extreme heat, humidity and constant insect bites.

Stage 3: survival and evasion

Those who remain are abandoned alone in the wilderness. Over the next few days, they must forage for food, make their own shelter, and avoid capture by army units.

Stage 4: back to school

Special Forces troopers need to master new skills, such as handling explosives...

...and parachute jumping.

Stage 5: coping with capture

One of the final tests is a brutal interrogation course. Instructors teach soldiers how to keep silent under torture...

...then try to break their spirits by persuading them that they are failures who should quit. Only the truly determined can cope.

Winning the badge

After more than six months of tests, successful soldiers are finally accepted into the SAS regiment. They wear a badge emblazoned with a flaming sword...

...and follow the famous SAS motto: 'Who dares, wins.'

Tarzan assault course

To join the Royal Marines, every volunteer must complete the notorious Tarzan assault course in under 13 minutes, wearing kit that weighs 14.5kg (32lbs).

Special Forces from all over the world come to the UK to try the Tarzan course.

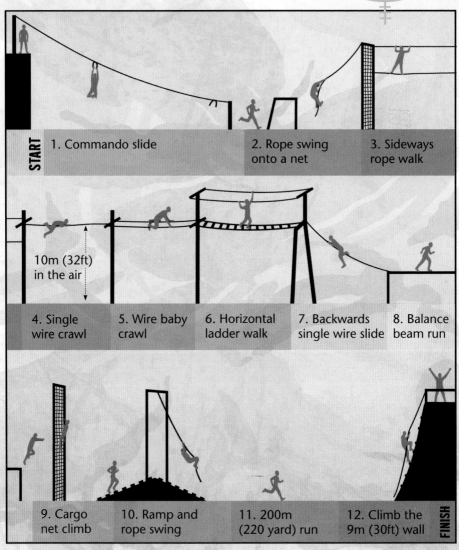

START

1. Commando slide

2. Rope swing onto a net

3. Sideways rope walk

10m (32ft) in the air

4. Single wire crawl

5. Wire baby crawl

6. Horizontal ladder walk

7. Backwards single wire slide

8. Balance beam run

9. Cargo net climb

10. Ramp and rope swing

11. 200m (220 yard) run

12. Climb the 9m (30ft) wall

FINISH

Royal Marine commandos tackle the single wire crawl at the Commando Training ground in Lympstone, UK.

Legion of the lost

One of the most famous SF units is the French Foreign Legion. It was formed in 1831 as a refuge for soldiers from any country who wanted to start a new life. Volunteers take on a new name, and swear an oath of loyalty to France.

A squadron of legionnaires marches through the Sahara Desert during a training exercise.

Some of the Legion's first battles were in French-occupied territories in the Sahara Desert in north Africa.

Special Forces on the internet

For links to websites where you can find out more about Special Forces from all over the world, go to the Usborne Quicklinks Website at **www.usborne-quicklinks.com** and enter the keywords: **special forces**.

White kepi hats protect soldiers from the fierce sun. Legionnaires still wear them today – when not in a combat zone.

The Foreign Legion was one of the first elite units to accept a female volunteer – British soldier Susan Travers, who joined during the Second World War.

Glossary

This glossary explains some of the words used in this book. If a word is written in *italic* type, it has an entry of its own.

assault rifle A hand-held gun with less range than a true *rifle*, but with the firepower of a *machine gun*.

assault vest A tough, combat jacket with pouches and clips for weapons and supplies.

automatic Any gun, such as a *machine gun*, that continually fires and reloads while the trigger is pressed.

bazooka A portable weapon that fires explosive rockets.

beret A soft cap worn by soldiers to identify their fighting unit.

Black Kit Combat dress for urban or night operations, with flameproof clothing, boots, helmet and gas mask.

camouflage The material or methods used to disguise soldiers and their equipment by blending in with their surroundings.

commando A soldier with special skills in making raids.

counter terrorism Work done to prevent or combat *terrorist* groups.

drop zone A designated landing area where *paratroopers* meet after a parachute jump.

extraction Getting soldiers away safely from a combat mission.

friendly A soldier or civilian supporting the same military forces.

frogman A military diver, with a wet suit, air supply and diving fins.

ghillie suit Camouflage clothing that covers the whole body.

grappling hook A spiked, metal pole tied to a rope. Soldiers throw the hook to clear tripwires and undergrowth or to climb up cliffs and other obstacles.

grenade An explosive device, thrown or fired from a launcher.

HAHO A high-altitude, high-opening parachute jump. The *paratrooper* opens his parachute immediately and steers slowly to a *drop zone*.

HALO A high-altitude, low-opening parachute jump. The *paratrooper* freefalls from the plane and opens his parachute less than a kilometer above the ground.

hijack To take control, by force, of a vehicle such as a plane or ship.

hostage A person held prisoner by a criminal such as a *hijacker*.

insertion Moving soldiers by boat, helicopter or other vehicle to the starting point of their mission.

kill house A training building that helps soldiers learn how to search and explore buildings safely. Sometimes called a shoot house.

laser A device that generates a powerful beam of light.

machine gun A gun that fires bullets automatically, as long as the gun's trigger is pressed.

mine An explosive designed to detonate when touched, often hidden just under the ground.

missile A weapon that is thrown or fired towards a target.

night vision Light intensification and heat imaging technology, used to help soldiers detect and track objects in low level light.

PJ Pararescue Jumper, a US Special Forces medic, trained to extract wounded or crashed *friendlies* from the battlefield.

paratrooper A soldier trained to jump into action using a parachute.

pointman The soldier at the head of a patrol in enemy territory.

rangefinder A *laser* device that measures distance to a target.

reconnaissance The work done to map and learn information about enemy territory and movements. Often known as recon.

rendezvous A designated meeting point, often used as a location for *extraction* at the end of a mission.

rifle A gun designed to be used against long range targets.

riot A street fight or violent disturbance involving a crowd.

roping To descend by lowering your body on a rope.

SEALs US Navy Special Forces trained to enter and complete missions by SEa, Air or Land.

semi-automatic Any gun that automatically reloads the chamber after the gun has been fired, but does not fire the new bullet until the trigger is pressed again.

sniper A military stalker and marksman.

submachine gun A light, hand-held version of a *machine gun*.

suppressor A tube, fitted to the muzzle of a gun, that changes the sound and reduces the noise of a shot. Sometimes called a silencer.

SWAT Special Weapons And Tactics. Originally the name for an elite unit within the Los Angeles Police Department, but commonly used to describe any elite police unit in the USA.

Tail-end Charlie The soldier bringing up the rear of a patrol through enemy territory.

terrorist A person who kills people, or blows things up, to make people afraid – often for a political reason.

Zodiac A nickname for a rigid inflatable assault craft used by marine units, taking its name from the manufacturer Zodiac.

Index

Acknowledgements

Every effort has been made to trace and acknowledge ownership of copyright. If any rights have been omitted, the publishers offer to rectify this in any future editions following notification. The publishers are grateful to the following individuals and organizations for permission to reproduce material on the following pages: (t=top, b=bottom, r=right, l=left)

cover SWAT officers © MILpictures by Tom Weber / Getty images; **p1** Special Forces frogmen on patrol in a rubber raiding craft © MILpictures by Tom Weber / Getty images; **p2-3** © PJF News / Alamy; **p4-5** © Peter Russell / Peter Russell Photography; **p6** © Peter Russell / Peter Russell Photography; **p7** © MILpictures by Tom Weber; **p8-9** © CPL Chris Moore, Commonwealth of Australia; **p10-11** © John Robert Young / Peter Russell Photography; **p16** © Leif Skoogfors / Corbis; **p18-19** © Maurizio Gambarini / epa / Corbis; **p20** © Hulton Archive / Stringer / Getty images; **p25** © Imperial War Museum H22831; **p26** © Hulton Archive / Stringer / Getty images; **p27** © Peter Russell / Peter Russell Photography; **p31** © Louie Psihoyos/Corbis; **p32-33** © Hulton Archive/Stringer / Getty Images; **p35** © Peter Russell / Peter Russell Photography; **p39** courtesy of Defenseimagery.mil and C. Todd Lopez, U.S. Defense Media Activity; **p40-41** © Jim Sugar / Corbis; **p41** (t and b) © Adrian Dean/F1ARTWORK; **p44-45** © MILpictures by Tom Weber; **p48** courtesy of Defenseimagery.mil and PH1 Arlo Abrahamson, U.S. Navy; **p49** courtesy of Defenseimagery.mil and Photographer's Mate 3rd Class Tony Spiker, U.S. Navy; **p50** (t) © Adrian Dean/F1ARTWORK; **p50** courtesy of Defenseimagery.mil and PH3 John Sullivan, U.S. Navy; **p51** courtesy of Defenseimagery.mil and Chief Photographer's Mate Andrew McKaskle, U.S. Navy; **p53** © Central European News / Europics; **p54** (t and b) © Adrian Dean / F1ARTWORK; **p54-55** © LA(Phot) Hamish Burke, Royal Navy, Crown Copyright; **p56** courtesy of Defenseimagery.mil and Mass Communication Specialist 3rd Class Robyn Gerstenslager, U.S. Navy; **p58** courtesy of Defenseimagery.mil and Spc. Christopher Hubert, U.S. Army; **p59** © MILpictures by Tom Weber / Getty images; **p64-65** © Gamma-Rapho via Getty Images; **p66** © Alexi Grachtchenkov / Peter Russell Photography; **p73** © Peter Russell / Peter Russell Photography; **p74-75** © Gamma-Keystone via Getty images.

Use of photos from Defenseimagery.mil does not imply or constitute
U.S. Department of Defense endorsement.

Additional illustrations by Zoe Wray, Anna Gould, Caroline Day and Lucy Wain
Series editor: Jane Chisholm   Series designer: Zoe Wray
Digital design by John Russell and Mike Olley   Picture research by Ruth King